Fact Finders®

What Is an Idiom

When IT'S AT Home?

by Emma Carlson Berne

Consultant: Robert L. McConnell, PhD

CAPSTONE PRESS
a capstone imprint

Fact Finders Books are published by Capstone Press,
1710 Roe Crest Drive, North Mankato, Minnesota 56003
www.mycapstone.com

Library of Congress Cataloging-in-Publication Data
Cataloging-in-publication information is available on the Library of Congress website.
978-1-5157-6388-8 (library binding)
978-1-5157-6393-2 (paperback)
978-1-5157-6405-2 (ebook PDF)

Editorial Credits:
Michelle Bisson, editor; Bobbie Nuytten, designer; Tracy Cummins, media researcher;
Laura Manthe, production specialist

Photo Credits:
Dreamstime: Ankevanwyk, 22; iStockphoto: Duncan Walker, 14, quisp65, 20;
Shutterstock: Andrey_Kuzmin, cover (right), Aratehortua, 27, BlueRingMedia, 12,
burnel1, cover (bottom), Complot, 10, Dmytro Zinkevych, 25 (bottom), dragon_fang,
24, easyshutter, 16–17, Eric Isselee, cover (middle), Erik Lam, cover (top left), Fabio
Balbi, 26 (top), Guzel Studio, 8, InesBazdar, 15, Kajano, 19, kalenderenk, 9, Ken Cook,
6 (top), kstudija, cover and interior design element, lineartestpilot, 18, mezzotint,
13, Michele Paccione, 6 (bottom), Natykach Nataliia, 21, nikitabuida, 25 (top),
Olga_Angelloz, 4, Rawpixel.com, 5, Rob Hyrons, cover (bottom left), Studio_G, 28;
Wikimedia: National Archives and Records Administration, 26 (bottom)

Printed in China.
010343F17

Table of Contents

CHAPTER ONE

Dressing the Chicken: What Is an Idiom?

Amelia Bedelia could not understand idioms. This fictional storybook maid "drew the drapes" with a sketchpad and a pencil. Mrs. Rogers, her boss, tells her to dress the chicken for dinner. Amelia Bedelia puts the bird in a little pair of green overalls. All of this makes for very funny fiction. Amelia Bedelia's antics also remind readers that understanding idioms is important. Idioms are useful and widely used.

An idiom is a phrase or a sentence that is a specific to the language and culture of the speaker or writer. A writer who is writing in English in the American South will use certain words or phrases. "I came up with her," she might say, meaning "I was raised with her." A writer writing in British English might use different words or phrases. For instance, Americans say and write "cross the road." British writers might say or write "go over the road." Both are correct, of course, but "go over the road" sounds odd to American ears, just as "cross the road" might sound odd to British ears.

Did You Know?

People often describe someone anxiously waiting as being on tenderhooks. The word is actually tenterhooks, and it comes from the days in which newly made fabric was stretched on a frame, with hooks—tenter-hooks—to dry.

Idioms sometimes, but not always, have a **figurative** meaning instead of a **literal** meaning. "Don't make a mountain out of a molehill" does not mean to create a hill with the piles of dirt that moles leave on your lawn. It means don't make a big deal out of something small. Here's another example: "It's raining cats and dogs." Quick! Does that mean a) dachshunds and Persians are literally falling from the clouds and creating doggy and kitty puddles on the ground? or b) It's raining very hard. If you can't answer that question, you may not be a native speaker of English, in which case you get a free pass.

Another example is a phrase you use when you are out of the house. An American might say he or she is "not at home." But a native Brit might say that he or she is "from home." There is no reason why one should say "at home" versus "from home." It's just the way each of our versions of English have evolved.

Buried Idioms

Often, idioms can be buried in regular sentences. **Phrasal verbs** are idioms as well. These figurative verbs often stump nonnative English speakers. For instance, you might bring the matter up at a business meeting. You're not literally lifting something from the floor. Or a person might be cut out for a particular job. No scissors involved—that person is simply right for the job. Someone who's had a bad experience might bounce back. No jumping, no ricocheting off a surface. Or how about egging someone on? No eggs are actually involved. The phrase means to **goad** someone into doing something—usually something foolish. The list of phrasal verbs is practically infinite, but it's colorful language like this that keeps our writing bright. Often though, phrasal verbs are overused and tired—they become **clichés** and lose some of their effectiveness.

figurative—expressing one thing in terms normally used for another

literal—following the ordinary or usual meaning of the words

phrasal verb—group of words that work as a verb; phrasal verbs can be idioms

goad—to urge something

cliché—phrase or expression that has been used many times

Idioms vs. Clichés

Idioms and clichés are sometimes linked. Clichés can be, and often are, idioms. And some, but not all, idioms are clichés. "Her hair was as black as night," is a clichéd way of describing something very black, for instance.

When used well, idiomatic phrases can add a fresh slant to your writing. "He's as tough as woodpecker lips." Brilliant, right? Fresh and weird. Here's another one: "He was off like a dirty shirt." Idioms can take a specific image and slam it into the reader's brain. They make the reader laugh unexpectedly or blink in surprise. Idioms give writers job security. Robots can't create idioms.

TRY IT OUT!

Write three sentences that include idioms. Then rewrite those sentences, removing the idioms but **retaining** the original meaning.

retain—to keep something

Any nonnative English language learner will tell you that our language, with all of its nonsensical spellings and weird sentence construction, is a headache to learn. And idioms don't make things any easier. There's no rule for them. You have to learn each idiom individually. And you have to get them exactly right. Reversing the words can mark you as a nonnative speaker. Raining dogs and cats? Sounds strange, right? That's because idioms have a certain rhythm and sequence to them, like poetry.

And every language has idioms. "Don't judge a book by its cover" is familiar to native English speakers. In French, a familiar idiom is, "I can do this *les doights dans le nez*," or "fingers in the nose," meaning "I can do this so easily that I can do it with my fingers in my nose." Idioms are hard to translate, and sometimes hard to understand. But they make our writing unique and flavorful. During periods of war, suspected spies posing as Americans have been asked to repeat American idioms as a test. The reasoning: only real Americans would be able to identify idioms from his or her native country.

Idiom vs. Literal Meaning

IDIOM	LITERAL MEANING	IF IDIOMS WERE REAL LIFE
I wouldn't be caught dead.	I would never do that.	I'm in a coffin, hoping to evade capture.
Pull the wool over her eyes.	Fool her.	Get some of this soft, puffy fleece. Now make it into a woolly blindfold, ok?
Elvis has left the building.	The matter is over. Everything has been decided.	Elvis Presley, the dead rock-and-roll singer, is not in this building. In fact, he is in the cemetery.
You hit the nail on the head.	You exactly understand the matter.	Good work with that hammer! You precisely whacked the protruding nail.
Don't cut corners.	Don't do a bad job to save time or money.	Measure out each piece of wood exactly, okay? If it says one inch, you measure and cut one inch.
Back to the drawing board!	Time to start over with new ideas.	Time to return to the large, flat board I use for drawing!
Time to hit the sack!	Time to go to bed!	It's time to take my fist and punch a large cloth bag!

11

CHAPTER TWO

A Stitch in Time:
Idioms and History

Many idioms are examples of figurative language. But they didn't start out this way. They started out as literal words. The phrasing was **succinct**, perhaps. Maybe someone famous said those words, perhaps in a public setting. Maybe it was a particularly clever or poetic way to express an idea. Whatever the reason, the phrase caught on.

For instance, "kicked the bucket" means died, not literally kicking over a mop pail. Where did it come from? Most scholars agree that the phrase comes from the practice of hanging a slaughtered animal, like a pig, upside down from a beam. The beam was called a bucket. An animal might sometimes kick after slaughter— striking the bucket. Over time, the literal meaning disappeared, perhaps as farming became less common, but the colorful phrase or sentence hung on.

The way we use it now, the phrase "white elephant" means a cumbersome gift or possession no one really wants. Originally, it did mean white elephants. In Thai history before the 20th century, white-colored elephants were highly prized. A king might give a white elephant to someone as a sign of that person's worth. English and European writers noticed this custom. They made up a story about it: that giving a white elephant was actually a way to punish someone. The animals were rare and prized, but also expensive to take care of. It wasn't really a gift anyone wanted. And an idiom was born.

succinct—to speak or write clearly without wasted words

Shakespeare's Idioms

The English language's most famous playwright and poet is William Shakespeare. Shakespeare lived in England from 1564 until 1616. Shakespeare is the source of many, many idioms. His poetry and plays were immensely popular and the music and playfulness of his words captivated his audience. It's no surprise that so many of his words have hung on.

Idioms Everywhere

All languages contain idioms. And they're all different. The Germans, for example, say "Tomaten auf den Augen haben." That means, "You have tomatoes on your eyes." It means someone is not seeing what others are seeing. Or if you are in Sweden and you're concerned about a test, your mother might say, "Det är ingen ko på isen," or "there's no cow on the ice." A cow standing on a frozen pond would be very dangerous and serious—the cow could fall through the ice and die. So saying "there's no cow on the ice" means "there's no great emergency." And in France, if you have flunked a test, you might mutter to yourself, "Les carottes sont cuites!" That means, "The carrots have been cooked." In other words, there's no sense in crying over spilt milk.

Maybe you've been in an awkward new social situation. No one really knows each other and no one is talking. You can suggest the group play a game to "break the ice." You probably didn't know you were quoting Shakespeare, but you were! In his play *The Taming of the Shrew*, the character named Tranio talks to a character named Hortensio about a plan to marry a woman:

> *If it be so, sir, that you are the man,*
>
> *Must stead us all, and me amongst the rest,*
>
> *And if you break the ice and do this feat,*
>
> *Achieve the elder, set the younger free*
>
> *For our access, whose hap shall be to have her*
>
> *Will not so graceless be to be ingrate.*

"You're the one who can help us all," Tranio says. "You can start us off on this interaction." In other words, Tranio thinks that Hortensio can "break the ice."

How about "wild-goose chase"? It means a fruitless hunt for something, but did you know the phrase originated in that ultimate love story, *Romeo and Juliet*? That's right. Romeo and his best buddy Mercutio are being silly with each other, bantering back and forth the way guys do, and Mercutio says, "Nay, if our wits run the wild-goose chase, I am done, for thou hast more of the wild-goose in one of thy wits than, I am sure, I have in my whole five. Was I with you there for the goose?" Of course, Mercutio doesn't mean to literally run after a wild, runaway goose. He means that this search is going to be pointless.

Other **iconic** texts have contributed their own fair share of idioms. The Bible gives Shakespeare a run for his money (ding! Idiom related to horse racing!) "Eye for an eye"? "Cross to bear"? "Bite the dust"? That's right—those are all from the Bible. Our iconic texts continue to give our language life and color.

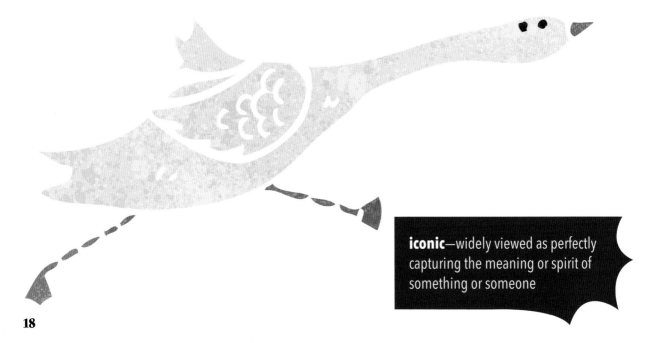

iconic—widely viewed as perfectly capturing the meaning or spirit of something or someone

TRY IT OUT!

Write down as many idioms as you can think of that include animals, such as "until the cows come home." Try to come up with at least five.

CHAPTER THREE

Make That Idiom
Work for You

So now we know that a cliché is an idiom that's overused. Idioms are often inserted unthinkingly into writing and speech because that's just the way we say certain things. But just because some idioms are comfortable or tired doesn't mean that idioms have no place in your writing. To the contrary, idioms can add color and fun. An idiom can get a big idea across in a few choice words. A strange idiom, like "chew the fat," or a funny idiom, like "when pigs fly," can snag the reader's attention, make him or her laugh out loud, or say an internal, "ahhh, yes!"

TRY IT OUT!

Take these three popular idioms and change them into new idiomatic phrases—extra points for humor and absurdity. For example, "raining cats and dogs" might be changed to "pelting petunias and peacocks."

Her lips were red as a rose.

Take it with a grain of salt.

That's the best thing since sliced bread!

But idioms are like salt—a little bit sprinkled just right adds that little kick of flavor you were missing. Too much salt? Your scrambled eggs are **inedible**. For instance, imagine that you wrote:

> *"Gosh, I'm all thumbs today!" Melanie declared, after knocking over her coffee.*
>
> *"Maybe you bit off more than you could chew," Darryl commented. "After all, you are trying to do the crossword in pen."*
>
> *"You can say that again," Melanie agreed. "You know what? I've got no skin in this game." She pitched the pen out the window. "After all, I always say, in for a penny, in for a pound." And she threw the coffee cup out the window as well.*

A Different Version

The story on the previous page is silly. Still, Melanie and Darryl's insistence on piling on idioms makes them sound as if they are brainless. Now, compare what they said before with this version:

> *"Whoops!" Melanie grabbed for her coffee cup, but it was too late. The brown liquid spread across the table, soaking Darryl's paper.*
>
> *"Maybe you're trying to do too much, dear," Darryl said, letting his paper drip over the sink. "After all, it would take a braver person than I to do the crossword in pen."*
>
> *"Oh, Darryl, why are you always right?" Melanie crossed her arms on her chest and scowled. "It kind of makes me hate you a little."*
>
> *Darryl wisely kept quiet and after a moment, Melanie sighed. "You know what? I'm through torturing myself." She opened up the window and pitched the crossword and the pen into the garden. They landed in the dahlias. Melanie stared at them a moment. "Why not?" she muttered and pitched the coffee cup out too.*

This version gets the story across without heavy **reliance** on idioms. It uses other language, such as descriptive words, more precise dialogue, and action verbs, to create pictures in the reader's mind.

inedible—not safe for eating

reliance—dependence on someone or something

CHAPTER FOUR

Idioms Ahead:
The Future's So Bright

"Language is always evolving" is a sort of cliché in itself, but it's also true. We still use all sorts of words from Old English, which was spoken before 1100. Eke (to get the most out of something by using it carefully) or sleight (the use of cunning, as in "sleight of hand") are examples of Old English words that we still use.

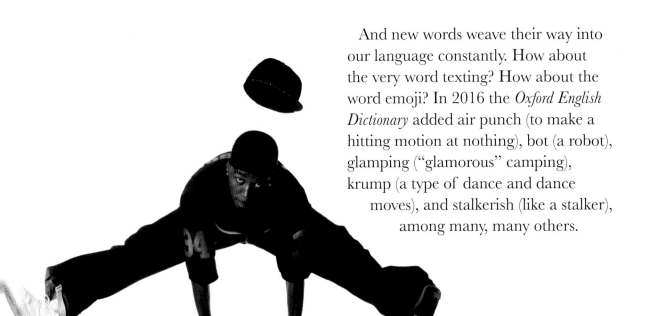

And new words weave their way into our language constantly. How about the very word texting? How about the word emoji? In 2016 the *Oxford English Dictionary* added air punch (to make a hitting motion at nothing), bot (a robot), glamping ("glamorous" camping), krump (a type of dance and dance moves), and stalkerish (like a stalker), among many, many others.

Idioms aren't always composed of words. Punctuation can function as a sort of idiom as well. Have you seen anyone Do. This. Online. Ever? Separating each word with a period to add emphasis to a point is pretty effective. How about putting a picture or a link up on social media and writing simply "THIS."

Did You Know?

Have you heard of committing yourself to something as unpleasant as "biting the bullet"? This idiom once was exactly what it sounds like. On 19th century battlefields, the doctor might give you an actual lead bullet to bite on before he amputated your leg. Bonus fact: You would bite on the bullet so you wouldn't bite off your own tongue!

Emojis as Idioms

EMOJI	LITERAL MEANING
	Love you! Kisses!
	Fist bump! We can do this!
	I'm laughing so hard, I'm crying!
	This is silly, what I'm saying right now.
	I'm pretty embarrassed.
	You're strong, or I'm strong.
	Oh no! I'm scared! or, This is very bad!
	We're together on this, I'm with you.

Idioms vs. Slang

There is a difference, though, between idioms and slang. Slang refers to words that are very casual, and are used in certain situations—such as when you are with your friends. Teachers usually don't allow slang in student writing. They usually do allow idioms. However, certain phrases and emojis can be considered modern idioms. Texting your friend "LOL" is more pithy and sharp than spelling out the entire phrase. When you're furious at your mother, a frowning face emoji on your phone says all you need to say. On the other hand, your mother will probably want a little more explanation!

Sometimes, older people feel anxious about how they think young people are messing up the language. Some people feared the telephone was going to destroy writing. And while it's true that the way we write and speak now is quite different from how our 19th century ancestors did, it's also true that the English language is as alive and rich as it's ever been. We add new words, we discard old ones, we hang onto others—just as we've always done. Idioms show up, they turn into clichés, they fade away, and new ones are created. Hearing new idioms can be exciting, but it's just another sign that our language is alive and evolving.

Glossary

cliché (klee-SHAY)—phrase or expression that has been used many times

figurative (FIG-yur-eh-tiv)—expressing one thing in terms normally used for another

goad (GOHD)—to urge something

iconic (EYE-kon-ik)—widely viewed as perfectly capturing the meaning or spirit of something or someone

inedible (in-ED-eh-buhl)—not safe for eating

literal (LIT-ur-uhl)—following the ordinary or usual meaning of the words

phrasal verbs (FRAZ-uhl VURB)—group of words that work as a verb; phrasal verbs can be idioms

reliance (ri-LYE-anse)—dependence on someone or something

retain (ri-TAYN)—to keep something

succinct (suh-SINKT)—to speak or write clearly without wasted words

Read More

Grammar and Punctuation. Collins Easy Learn. New York: HarperCollins, 2015.

Fielder, Heidi. *The Know-Nonsense Guide to Grammar: An Awesomely Fun Guide to the Way We Use Words!* Know Nonsense Series. Lake Forest, Calif.: Walter Foster Jr., 2017.

Sabra, Ponn, and **Habeeba Husain**. *Poetic Puns: Grammar Made Fun*. Ponn Press, Amazon Digital Services, 2013.

Critical Thinking Questions

1. What is the difference between an idiom and a cliché? Provide an example by using each in a paragraph.

2. This text provides many examples of idioms. How do examples help the reader understand the author's meaning?

3. What is your favorite idiom found in this text? Explain why you like this particular idiom.

Internet Sites

Use FactHound to find Internet sites related to this book.

Visit *www.facthound.com*

Just type in 9781515763888 and go!

Index